What Matters

Young Writers and Artists Speak Out

DaVinn Richardson
Age 13

What Matters

Young Writers and Artists Speak Out

Glide Word Press
Glide Foundation
San Francisco, California

Dedicated to

Megan Furth
Ntombi Howell
June Jordan
Alan Tinker

Glide Word Press
330 Ellis Street
San Francisco, CA 94102

Janice Mirikitani, Editor
   What Matters. *Young Writers and Artists Speak Out*

First Paperback Edition, 2004
ISBN 0-9622574-3-5
Publisher Cataloging-in-Publication Data
   1. Children's writings, American
   2. American literature–California–San Francisco
   3. American literature–21st century
   4. San Francisco (Calif.)–Literary collection

Printed by: Cenveo, San Francisco, CA

Front cover collage by: George W. Briggs IV, Amy Ung, Jennifer Mong
Rocio Montes, Mauricio Rangel, Linda Wong, Kristy Nguyen, Lilian Mong
Evelynn Ly, Troy Talton, Isabella Talton, Willie Talton, Cheery Huang,
Darell Davis

Acknowledgements

Janice Mirikitani, Editor

Joyce Hayes, Creative Coordinator
Candace Snyder, Project Coordinator
Sandra Shuhert, Graphic Designer
Jane Fox, Technical Coordinator
Shawn O'Docharty, Art Coordinator
Ted Seymour, Photography Instructor
Alain McLaughlin, Photographer of cover graphic
LaKisha Bridgewater, Project Intern

Poetry Instructors
Lucinda Ray, Derek Lassiter, Ian Atkinson

Assistants
Karen Junker, Hilary Near, Mike McNeil

Youth Editorial Committee
Classy Martin, Sophia Valiente,
Monica Reese, Dawn Monanau, Anastasia Ross,
Donald Murphy, Djourn Elarmes, Rashard Hoggs

Special thanks to:
Reverend Cecil Williams
Pastor Douglass Fitch
Rita Shimmin
Bruce Williams
The Glide Board of Trustees
Dr. Maya Angelou
Isabel Allende

Generous Contributions from our Donors:
The Furth Family Foundation
The Tides Foundation
Glide Rosevelt Winchester Fund
Linda & David Mantel
Zellerbach Family Fund
Isabel Allende Foundation
Alexander and June Maisin Foundation

Table of Contents

1   The Skin I Am In

Poets	*Artists*

Table of Contents

2 Home Cookin'

Poets	Artists

Table of Contents

5 Create A World

Poets   Artists

6 Can't Do It Alone

Foreword

"What Matters" has been a five year journey culminating in this anthology of poetry, prose and visual art created by young people who have participated in Glide's programs. Glide is a spiritual home that provides opportunities to empower, educate, liberate and uplift people of all ages, a vision of Cecil Williams and Janice Mirikitani which began forty years ago. Life supporting programs in the areas of health, human services, housing, mental health, counseling, recovery, recreation, education, mentoring, the arts, job training, and spirituality continue today to wrap around each individual child, youth, and adult, opening doors of choice and widening the paths to a community of compassion.

LaKisha Bridgewater, a student at UC Berkeley who worked at Glide Church as a 2003 summer intern on this anthology project, wrote:

> *"The youth...entrusted me with silent prayers sitting in their hearts that revealed themselves in poetic form...they held mirrors that reflected my childhood image undistorted and understood...they highlighted the ailments they see in their community and reminded me how important it is that I take a stand...Our children have stories to tell...they see the need for changes in our world and they dare to be those changes with our help..."*

Our youth and children tell us **What Matters** to them. Do we listen?

What Matters
> *Life. Taking a stand.*
>> Here are the mirrors which reflect ourselves, "undistorted and understood..." Contained in these pages are the realities of young people who desire to shape a world in ways that reflect all of our hopes and dreams.

What Matters
> *Naming Our Names. The words that define who we really are.*
>> There is great power in being able to name who we are, what we care about and where we come from. Courage comes from the pride we take in our humanity despite the stereotypes, name calling, the "racial and generational imprinting" that occur when we find ourselves marginalized because of social and economic injustices.

What Matters

Justice. Experiences that our children witness and are touched by.

    We must listen to their stories, see with their eyes what they see, because it is in our hearing that they are validated and empowered. It is in our compassion and love that we all – writer and reader – are made more whole.

What Matters

Change. The messages of our young people who challenge us with their truth.

    We are transformed if we dare to receive the truth that requires us to perceive ourselves and others more fully. We are enriched. We can act. Our world expands.

What Matters

Soul. The spirit to persevere.

    Here are dandelions growing out of concrete,
amidst the broken bottles, discarded needles.

Wildflowers of wondrous hues,
Subtle fragrance,
Delicate petals, still.
Please handle with care.

Each morning bright faces
Turn to follow the sun,
Hopeful as pollen,
We will survive this day.
We will go further.

What Matters

Read about yourself
in these pages.
Partake of this courage.

–Janice Mirikitani
San Francisco Poet Laureate, 2000
Executive Director, Glide Foundation

1

...You look at me
And before you even
ask my name,
you say "What are you?"...

–Ashley

The Skin I Am In

I love the skin I am in
It is brown in the bright sunshine
It is pale in the snow
Then there is that dark shadow of me
That follows me everywhere I go.
When I am clean I sparkle like gold
I will love the skin I am in when I get old.

Sophia Valiente
Age 12

Maria Choy
Age 9

Radio Tunes

Blue
       Radio
              tunes
       loud
             Music
Bumping
       Ears
Rhymes
       flow
       always
             and
                  forever...

Sophia Valiente
Age 13

Pit Bull

My animal's eyes
will be brown like mine
and he will be buff
like me.

Ernesto Valiente
Age 13

I Try

I try to be a maple tree on Millwood Street
I try to be ice cream singing in the freezer
I try to be a dolphin with soft sound
I like to go to school on Wednesdays
I am a green, blue and yellow circle
I try to have wings that go shhhh
I try to sleep in my spring bed
That's beautiful when I'm angry
I try to be a hurricane in the south
I try to be jewels singing, acting and playing
In Hawaii
I try to be rain on a high mare
And an angel at 5:00
I try to be a teacher in May
My life has freedom
My life has God and the Bible

Kyra Hoge–Habekoss
Age 9

Crystal Hayden
Age 15

Black

Black, serene night
The distinct color of beautiful
The divine color of strength
Pure & dark like the passion of love
Wild & free in it's naturality
Black, the color of me

Anastasia Ross
Age 17

Music of Poetry

Poetry is the colored leaves that fall from
the rusted trees in autumn.
Poetry is like a huge puzzle that can
always be put together the right way even
if it does not make any sense at all.
Poetry is the moon that the grey wolves sing their lullabies to.
The music of poetry can only be heard at night
when you think that you
cannot hear anything
at all.

Cierra Crowell
Age 10

Reach for the Stars

Reach for the Stars
With all your might
Jump on the moon...
Hold on tight!

Kylie Woodward-Sollensnes
Age 7

Disability

You can label me
With a disability.
Don't call me stupid.

I may think before I speak
So what I say may be too deep.
So DON'T call me stupid.

I'm a pearl of a girl
Not an insult to the world
You might think you're smart
But you don't know what I know

Let me tell you something clear,
People have disabilities:

Like Whoopie Goldberg and Tom Cruise
Charles Schwab, Mayor Newsom too.

Albert Einstein, did you know that?
Walt Disney and Cher and that's a fact

Harry Belafonte, Alexander Graham Bell,
Danny Glover and Winston Churchill.

Helen Keller was deaf and blind
But for so many people she turned on the light.

Frida Kahlo could not walk
But used her wounds to make her art.

Marla Runyan ran her race blind
Magic Johnson speaks his mind.

Did you know Chris Burk, the TV star?
He's got Down's Syndrome and he's gotten far.

Stephen Hawking, Patty Duke
Itzhak Perlman just to name a few.

So when you see me,
Don't look down at me, look up,
Because there's a lot to learn
From a person like me
With a learning disability.

You heard it from me.
I'm Tiffany.

Tiffany Haynes
Age 17

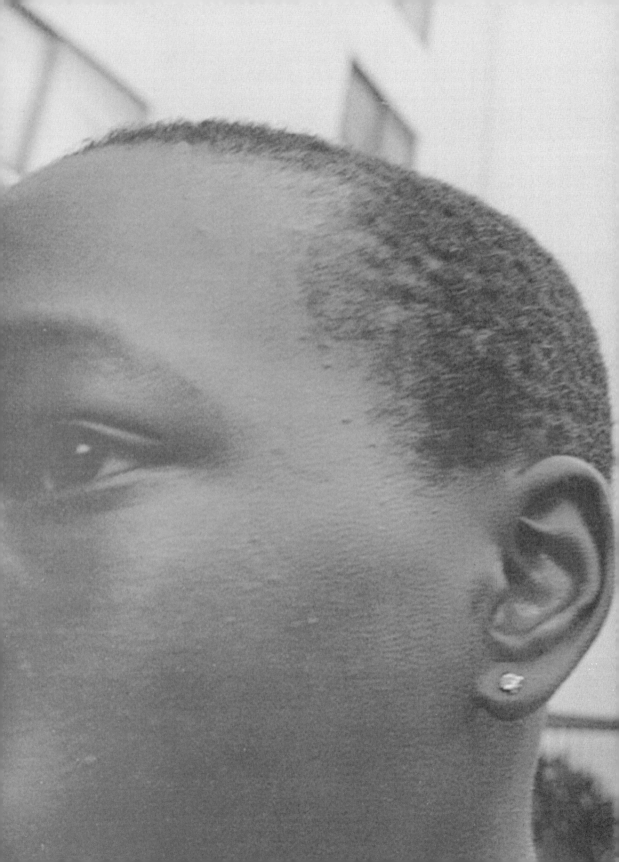

Clinton's Rap

Clinton Washington is my name
Going to school is my game
I like that Math and English too
Music and P.E. are fun to do
I want to be something one of these days
And get a good job that really pays

The teachers I know are true right through
If you listen, you can learn a lot too
Sometimes it's hard and that's no lie
But if I do what's right the time goes by
Before you know it I'm ahead of my game
And feeling good about me is my claim to fame

Clinton Washington
Age 13

DaVinn Richardson
Age 13

Dreams

The sky is blue, and the grass is green
And when I hear you sing
It's like a dream come true
When I see you
Looking so beautiful
And I say that because I love you!

Keeana Thompson
Age 11

Isabella Talton
Age 8

The Sun Is Rising

Its 5:30… the sun is rising
I'm trying to beat the sun before it rises
I'm trying to get up, get dressed
And run down to the beach to see the sunrise.
If I don't make it then I won't see the sunrise
And I will have to catch it tomorrow morning
So I race down to the beach
But then it happened
The sun rose… and I made it!
And I wasn't late, I made it
I wasn't late, I made it!
The sunrise was great and beautiful,
I loved it.
The sun was rising and I made it.

Anonymous

A YOUNG BLACK WOMAN

I AM A YOUNG BLACK WOMAN
Who can take care of herself.

I AM A YOUNG BLACK WOMAN
Who knows what she is doing
And doing things she never did before.

> Writing poetry,
> Singing,
> Getting good grades in school,
> Speaking up for myself,
> Telling people what's on my mind

I AM A YOUNG BLACK WOMAN
Who can defend herself and has the power.

I AM A YOUNG BLACK WOMAN
Who will one day wake up and be Somebody
Maybe a nurse or a poet.

I AM A YOUNG BLACK WOMAN
Who will keep walking and talking
No matter what people say.

I AM A YOUNG BLACK WOMAN
Who is here before you to say

Think about who you are
And what you are
And where you're going

A YOUNG BLACK WOMAN
Going into the future.

Classy Martin
Age 17

Crystal Hayden
Age 15

I Want To Be an Actress

I want to be an actress.
I want to do crazy things and
I want people to think I'm funny.

In the movies, I want everyone to like me.
I would not show off like some
People who are famous.

I want to respect other people,
And not be snob or mean,
If I were an actress.

Crystal Hayden
Age 11

Dreams

Once I dreamed I could fly.
I had beautiful red and gold wings.
My feathers were as soft as silk.

Kylie Woodward-Sollesnes
Age 8

Kelvin Richardson
Age 9

Just Ashley

I'm not black enough to be black…
Yet I'm not white enough to be white…

You look at me,
And before you even ask my name,
You say, "What are you?"

I have flesh and blood,
Just like you
I have two eyes, a nose and a mouth,
Just like you
I bleed, I cry, I laugh, I smile
Just like you
I am young woman, a person,
Just like you

Yes, my nose may be broader, or maybe more thin
My skin is lighter or perhaps a shade darker
But red blood still runs through my veins, as through yours

Some women hate my mother because she,
"Took their man"
And some men hate my father because he,
"Took advantage of her"

I am the product of sin,
In the eyes of some.

They talk to me in curiosity,
Surprised when they have something in common…
With a Mulatto girl.

I must be adopted
Or maybe a friend
You think to your self
As I grasp my WHITE mother's hand

I don't want your sympathy
Save your pity for another soul

For I know that I am beautiful
Just the way that God made me

Not black and not white,
But just Ashley.

Ashley Forbes
Age 18

Ernesto Valiente
Age 13

A Rainy Day

Drip, Drop, Drip, Drop
Falling like diamonds from the sky
Drip, Drop, Drip, Drop
Falling like teardrops in my eye
Drip, Drop, Drip, Drop
Beads of pearls fall with morning dew
Drip, Drop, Drip, Drop
Showers of words saying I love you

Jazmyne Thompson
Age 11

Ocean

Ocean has water.
Ocean has fish.
Ocean has turtles.
Mix it all together,
you make an ocean.

Kiara Bowling
Age 9

Dolphin

My favorite animal is gray, big,
cute and smart.
It loves people
and it has a good heart.
It's eyes are sometimes brown,
browner than dirt.
Play too rough with it
and you will get hurt.
These animals are caring, peaceful
and good companions too.
Spend time with this creature
and it will love you.

Crystal Hayden
Age 11

Strong Black Man

My name is Recco Payne and I am a strong black man.

Dr. King was a strong black man.
He sent powerful messages through his hand.

I have only been on this earth for seven years.
The work Dr. King has done brings lots of cheer.

Like Cecil Williams
He brought people of all colors together.

On this day of celebration
Let it bring us spirit forever.

Recco Miguel Darcell Payne
Age 7

Mama

My Mama is the best
Much better than the rest
I see her in the twisting ocean
She gives me comfort of
Jasmine and lavender lotion
Much beautiful too
This poem shows that
I love you.

Kiara Bowling
Age 8

Out

When you say out,
What does it mean to you?
Well, to me is a very powerful word
in my experience.
Well, out for me was,
Get out you're mixed.
And maybe, get out,
You're ugly.
Out can be a very meaningful word,
Even if you use it in a good way,
You might hurt someone's feelings.

Patrice Moananu
Age 12

Maria Choy
Age 9

Nigger

I can't be your dog
I can't be your cat
I can't be your friend
I can't be your house

I can't be your pen
I can't be your paper
I can't be your car
I can't be your mouse

I can't be your uncle
And buy you shoes when he doesn't
I can't be your brother
I can't be your cousin

I can be bigger, but I can't
Be your NIGGER

Inocente Estella
Age 14

My Name

My name is Clinton.
I don't know who named me Clinton,
I think my dad named me it,
Because his name is Clinton.
If I would change my name
It would be Jesse,
Because it sounds COOL!

Clinton Washington
Age 13

A Player

A player is a pimp dogging brother that
Can't get no love from me,
Well that's what I think,
What about you?

Patrice Moananu
Age 12

DaVinn Richardson
Age 13

Absurd Growth

Some flowers
wilt
before autumn…
fade into sunset
recede into memory
vanish away

Some flowers
bend to the sun
thrive on light
creep higher
when the moon calls
blossom for themselves

This flower
shivers
in morning breeze
quaking in moments
afraid
dares
To Be

This flower
knows too many shadows
yet denies
ever being out
climbs up terraces
posts along the way

This flower
is bright
in a mellow way
always searching
to define
its color

This flower
Is alone
less than it thinks
on the nights
when autumn arrives
leaves turn and fall
to this flowers breath absorbed in its
ironic beauty of confusion

This flower
thrives on, hidden in creation
through mind.
Petals shower
this aching plant to death
over trying too hard
reaching for the wrong rain

Tanene Allison
Age 18

The Rainbow Tree

Once there was a tree
A beautiful tree.
It had five different colors in it:
                Red, purple, green
                Yellow and brown.
Red represents love,
Purple is beauty,
Yellow represents sunlight
Green and brown represent nature.

Kylie Woodward-Sollesnes
Age 8

Rose

Very beautiful
Simple yet absolutely
Perfect in all ways

Jackie Groffman
Age 13

What Matters: You

What matters my family because they encourage me to be
what I want to be!
What matters my church because they love me.
What matters my mother because she loves me and made
me.
What matters I matter because I'm alive.
What matters this poem because I get to express
myself.
What matters the world but most of all you!

BryeeAnna Belmar
Age 8

Sophia Valiente
Age 14

Tofu Mountain

My rock is a tofu mountain
Along with the Great Wall of China
Smooth, snowy, slippery, good
No people starve
Because
If you take a bite of my mountain
It's very tasty
It never rains water
Only soy sauce
Animals of hunger come to my rock
At anytime
I bet any one of you have been to my rock
In a dream of happiness.

Kyra Hoge-Habekoss
Age 8

The Person Across From Me

Reminds me of
A person on a T.V. show
'2 Guys a Girl and a Pizza Place'
Who always trips over something,
                                            even her own shoe lace

Long and silky hair
Makes you want to stare
Stare for so long you can't stand it anymore
Milky, creamy, funny looking skin
It makes you want to ask her
"Where have you been?"

And her round forehead
So soft, clean, and smooth
It makes you want to sing…the blues

Classy Martin
Age 16

They Treat You like Dirt

They treat you like dirt because of your color;
You say that it doesn't really matter.
You let them push you down and down,
You let them wear your own crown.
Prove to them that you aren't nothing,
Prove to them that you are really something
Tell me, are you satisfied with living your life cheap?
I could keep letting you weep.
You always tell me to stand up tall,
But how can I, when you aren't at all?
You need to stand up high,
So that the whole world can see you shine.
Don't look at me that way, like I'm wrong
Because you are the reason I wrote this poem.

Cierra Crowell
Age 10

When I was writing this poem, I realized there are many voices that speak through me. These are all members of my family:

On The Question Of Race

They ask me to write down
My race

And I think
And I think
Very seriously

And consider writing down the truth
And have my answer read

I have a soldier
Who went to Normandy
To fight for justice

I have a woman
Killed in the gas chambers
Of Auschwitz

I have a man
Trying to teach me
The ancient Torah
Bedazzling me with his words

I have a woman
In San Francisco
Who feeds the poor
During the depression

I have two men
Eager to serve
This country
As Navy Seals

I have
So much
To be thankful for

They ask me to write down
My race
And I think
Very seriously

And consider
Writing down the truth
And have my answer read
I have the pain of
The Holocaust
Inside this body

I have the cheering
And excitement
Of the horse races
Inside this body

I have a teenage boy
From the richest part of Chicago
Who's the first-string quarterback
Inside this body

I have an abused woman
Who married her enemy
To get away
Inside this body

I have the
Heroes of America
And of the world
Inside this body

But I stop

And simply
Write down
White

*What Matters is: that I am more
than a checked box. I am a person.
And I am proud of who I am.*

Jackie Groffman
Age 14

Home Cookin'

Mama,
you smile through the pain...
Mama,
stop pretendin'...

–LaTeisha

Gangs

I spent all my life hoping
I could get jumped into a gang
So that I could be cool or what not.
Maybe if I were in a gang
I wouldn't get picked on or talked about.
I might meet friends and people
I could hang out with
and go to parties with.
Maybe even drive a car
at the age of 14 years young,
Smoking some weed,
drinking some nice cold wine.
Kicking it and chilling
and having a good time.

But "No!" I say
to myself over and over, dying.
No that won't be me,
yes it sounds nice and cool
But it's not a good road to go down.
I slowly walk away
from the gang I wanted to be in
Never, never will I think
That stupidly again!

So What Matters is:
You should show
your kids love
otherwise they might
look somewhere else for love.

Ernesto Valiente
Age 13

José Estella
Age 10

Are You In My Life?

Today it seems like you're not in my life,
Are you?
I can't tell, because you are acting unusual today.
What's the matter?
Did I do anything?
Can I help?
Tell me what's up cause you know I care for you.
You are like a shining star that lights up at night,
Brighter than any star that I have noticed.
You're like the moon,
The moon is just like you
Because the moon came from God
And you'll be one of the many last ones to leave Earth.
And you'll be the best of the best.

Classy Martin & Patrice Moananu
Ages 17 & 12

Untitled (4 now)

We sit under the stars,
Moon and the sky,
Sitting there with you is worthalifetime.
Laying in my bed watching T.V.
Sitting without you stings like a bee
I think about you all the time
You are my mind, soul and heart
When I'm in your tight warm embrace
I know we will never be apart.

Sophia Valiente
Age 13

Crystal Hayden
Age 15

Puppy

Cute.
Furry.
Licks a lot.
Brown or Black.
Small.
Purple eyes.
Pink eyes.
Hazel eyes,
Silver eyes.
When I'm sad
he knows
and he comforts me.

Christina Calloway
Age 11

His Story

Days you try to put into words seem to
Blur into emotion flawed with non-sense
I watch you try to make sense of it all
So you growl and you pout and you pull out your hair
You sing another man's song at the top of your lungs
Cause you can't find your own lyrics
And his sound good enough
But he sings without emotion while you
Feel every word.
It's just the way life goes
So hard to hold on, afraid to let go
The melody softens rough nature that
Clogs up your mind
Still you can't find a medium
A way to rid it all, well,
   I'm listening
Waiting for a sign
I know it's in you; it's just a matter of time
Before you realize your story
It's got a lot of special effects
And I don't mind watching

Lucinda Ray
Age 18

Love is a Southern Season

Love is the southern season to you and me.
I put my mind to what I want.
I can see things in my mind,

I can see Love.

I can have a pow wow in my mind.
I can do what I want.

Lynn Moananu Stills
Age 11

Maria Choy
Age 9

Cheetah, Tiger

When the tiger meets the cheetah
maybe it will eat it
if it didn't, he would say
it's my forest—get out of my way
If the cheetah didn't move
it would scratch his big spotted cheeks.

What if the orange tiger missed
and the quick young cheetah got pissed?
Two minutes later the cheetah and the
tiger were lovers forever.

Kelvin Johnson
Age 9

Love

Love is like a rainbow in the sky
the colors are much like people they live and die.

Love is happy and sometimes sad
Sometimes it hurt or even makes you mad.

Love is all around us each and every way
At night I pray for peace to begin each and every day.

Pokemon is my favorite past time, especially Pica-Chu
Even though they are pocket monsters, they're still my friends too.

As I grow up day after day
I will spread my love, along the way.

Recco Payne
Age 12

What Matters

What matters is not a question
That I get everyday
So I'll have to think before I say
Every night before I pray,
I make sure the woman who raised me is okay
In her soft bed, where she lays
I am glad to say my grandmother raised me
From when I was a young child to now
When I am a teen and a little crazy
Even when she's stressed out

I am still her baby.

Patrice Moananu
Age 12

Love

Love laces itself in our hearts & our lives
And no one can put out our flame of passion
As people in the world we know how to
Play drums & dance & sing hallelujah
For we are free to be ourselves
And nothing can cease our celebration.

Lucinda Ray
Age 18

Clinton Washington
Age 13

All about Me G.J.B. IV

I'm from the city of raiders
Where O G's wear gators
And young bloods stay bumping in all the scrapers
Brothers stay wearing locks and braids on top
And, "like what" is what we say when we're feeling joyful today

But dancing
Man we have a whole nother taste
Swinging our head and moving our face
And yes we keep our fresh JO's laced

Now I have to speak about my family
I have a little bad brother and a big bad mother
Us together are a family of no other

My mom is a doctor and my dad is in construction
For a middle class family they have to put food on the table to function

My little brother is jive and his attitude is so alive
He goes to Saint Leo's and sometimes asks my mom "Can I drive?"

Now if it wasn't for my family
I wouldn't be able to breathe
Growin' up in the hard Streets of the East
You both made it Possible for me to achieve
What I do now is because of you
I'm proud.

George James Bouie IV
Age 16

Tough Lady

A tough lady is not the one who is in fights all the time
A tough lady is the woman who is down with her kids
A tough lady is the one up before daylight, ironing school clothes, cooking breakfast
Tough ladies go to bed after everyone else is asleep
Tough ladies take care of 6 or 7 kids, while no one takes care of them

My grandma is a tough lady.

Dawn Moananu
Age 14

Sunshine

You are the sun for my
Day. You are the flower that I Love
So much. You are helpful and
Kind. You are my Heart . . . You
Are my mother.

George Briggs III
Age 16

The Road of Life Ain't Easy

Father I ask you this question
Why the inside of me hurts?
What is the point of livin'
When it feels like I've been cursed?

Son, pay attention
The road of life ain't easy
I may not come when you call,
But I'll be there when you need me.

You have to stand your ground
When the heat comes to strike
You have battle wounds and scars,
But you must keep up the fight
With all your might.

Put me first,
I'll guide you through the storm.
I gave you a gift; you say it's a curse
Remember warriors are born.

Son, Pay Attention
The road of life ain't easy.
I may not come when you call
But I'll be there when you need me.

Jesse Holford
Age 17

Sophia Valiente
Age 14

True Love

For my teacher whose son died

She wept as she lay in the wind.
She wept as she walked down the slow sidewalk.
She wept all night and day.
She tried to shut her eyes,
But it was too hard
For she had lost her true love.

Kylie Woodward-Sollesnes
Age 7

My Mama's Chocolate Cake

The shell cracks open upon the kitchen tile
I watch the yolk emerge from a perfect circle
So perfect it seems faulty
Like the eggs my mama would use
From the government food box
Even I, a 6 year old
Could taste the difference.
The taste of powered milk
Full of sour mishaps
That spilled out the tip of my Barbie cup
As I would blow bubbles through the straw

Seemed
Powdered bubbles never quite satisfied me
Like the right smooth milk
From the bosom of an anonymous cow

I pour the milk into a bowl
Search for another egg
Flour, chocolate
My arms struggle to mix it together

Now is time for the best part
I wrap my tongue around the spoon used to mix
Capture every stray clump of chocolate
Then grind it between my teeth

Final procedure
Let it bake
Spread the aroma of good cookin'
Throughout the house
Only this isn't government material

No, I'm never too good for mama's home chocolate cake
But for me, it's the same recipe
With different ingredients

Lucinda Ray
Age 18

Stop Pretending

Put a smile on your face, Put a twist in your waist,
Take you to that special place
Mama...........Stop Pretending

You smile in the rain; you smile through the pain,
You take happiness in vein
Mama...........Stop Pretending

Putting on a front for them folks, you have all the different hopes,
But you know you can never cope
Mama............Stop Pretending

You have all these problems, but smile in life,
You laugh at strife, But all this time,
You worried about bein' a good wife
Mama............Stop Pretending

Taking you on journeys of confused clouds,
You want to deal with the pain, but don't know how,
You keep your mouth shut, And look at you now
Mama.........Stop Pretending

I open my mouth, and you get upset,
You say you are fine. Wanna bet?
You say it, but I haven't seen you do anything yet
Mama…………..Stop Pretending

Hurt is what I see in your eyes, constantly you hear lies,
You yearn to know what he's feeling inside
Mama………….Stop Pretending

You never state what you feel,
All along I can tell this pain is real, and you are with him still
Mama………..Stop Pretending

You say he will be out of this home,
Even then he won't leave you alone.
All he does is complain and groan…………..
Please Mama…………Stop Pretending

La'Teisha Brathwaite
Age 12

José Estella
Age 10

Untitled

I'm angry
My Grandfather took me away from my mother...
she was going through issues

Now Agents
keep calling to speak to my mom
I tell them I don't know my mom

Is that a bad thing?

Alex Burke
Age 11

Mother Lying Sick in Bed

Dear Mom,

Why do you shed tears? Did I say everything? Well hell, all you had to do was keep your faith and God would do his will. I know you had your ups and downs and you wished you could have spent Valentines Day with us. But guess what Mom? We brought it to you, not tripping on whatever may happen. Just to know that you are happy makes my sickness from you not being home go all the way away.

I want you to know that we all love you, and will visit you every day. But when I get a call and they announce that you are dead, I don't know what the hell I am going to do, because damn truly I love you and with all of my heart and that is what my father said too.

After they pronounced you dead,
they called the next day,
saying you *weren't* dead.
I rushed down to the hospital
to see what the hell was going on

And as I ran into your room, I saw.
There you were,
more alive than anything in this world.
All I know is that you're my medicine man,
and I will always and forever
beware of an illness
that can be called death.

Dana Johnson
Age 16

Feelings

I'm feeling happy because my Dad
is out of the hospital.
He was sick so that's why I'm happy he's out.
I missed him.
When he came back, I gave him a big hug.

I love my Dad.
He takes care of me.
Makes sure I am not hungry
Makes sure I'm not cold
Makes sure I go to school and get a good education.

I'm going to go to college.
I'm going to graduate from college.

When I'm happy I smile sometimes.

Thinking about my Dad
Makes me smile.

Ashley Haynes
Age 10

Life

This life belonged to my mother
But when I was born, she gave it to me
Still
She won't let me live my life
I am entrapped in my mother's body
Please let me be and not what you want me to be
I want to be free
I want to be set free from this place that I live in
Please rescue me from this place I am in
Give me my LIFE!

La'Teisha N. Brathwaite
Age 12

#1 (untitled)

I took the money you were
going to use to buy shoes.

He is my new companion and
best friend.

But now you have no shoes
and I have a best friend.

Sophia Valiente
Age 13

Flying

I wish I was a blue jay
I would fly through the fluffy white clouds
I would flap my baby blue wings
Until I fell into the arms of my mama bird.

Kylie Woodward-Sollesnes
Age 8

Sophia Valiente
Age 14

How Is Yo' Life?

Say it again?
Yo' mama is sleeping with another man
Just to keep clothes on y'all back
And food in her 15 kids mouths
I said, "I wonder why yo' mamma got 15 kids?"
She said, "Well how is yo' life?"
I said, "It's not that usual,
but I keep it on the DL."

Patrice Moananu
Age 12

Under Couch

dark blackness

white and gray dust bunnies
cover a maple brown floor

I found my Mom's wedding ring

Sophia Valiente
Age 13

...because you give me
what I need,
I can grow through the weeds
and blossom...

–Dawn

At the Rec Center

I was watching a basketball game at the Rec Center.
During the game, a boy I knew was fouled
intentionally
                   several times
by another player on the opposite team.

My friend who got fouled said, "Watch out, blood."
The other player, a Cambodian, replied,
"I ain't no blood, cuzzz!"
And he fouled him again.

After the game, my friend came up to me and said,
"Forget that. I'm going to get a gun and shoot him
in the back of the head..."

He was so angry, so I told him to relax. It wasn't that serious…
Think about the consequences.
If he shoots someone, he will go to jail.

The consequences, look at consequences before making a decision.

A coward would take another person's life out of anger.

My friend calmed down and did not go get his gun.

Let peace begin with me. I know too many people who died due to violence.
I know a lot of people who are suffering and trapped due to drugs.

But **WHAT MATTERS** *is that i can be a strong individual and make the right decisions*
that determine my future. Self Respect and Self Determination can change the world.
That is what matters.

Jesse Holford
Age 18

Circumstance

I want to die, I don't wanna be here
I wish I never existed
If you live life through my eyes,
You will see how it's twisted.

I am a prince
I need to walk with the world on my shoulders
Or I can take an easy route and die as Jesse Holford

When my life is over
I want to look back and see I did my thang
BIG WHOPP DA KING
Of dis west coast rap game

My life ain't the same as his
Livin' in a city full of GIANTS
Stuff can get DANGEROUS

A FATHER DIES, and leaves his boy stranded
He wasn't a man yet
Mamma got a new boyfriend
So now the son gets abandoned

So now he's out on his own
Walking in the COLD
HE AIN'T GOT THE DOUGH
To CURE the stomach moan

He ready to run in a liquor store
To hit him up 4 a lot of stuff
Then run out with his hand
Clutched to his gun.

Right before he walks in da store
He dropped his mask
Bent down and picked up a scratcher
AND WON HELLA CASH!

*What Matters: even though you feel like
there's no escape from the darkness, you
just keep on walking and you stumble
on a flashlight.*

Jesse Holford
Age 18

Kelvin Richardson
Age 9

I'll Wish a Wish

I'll wish a wish; you'll wish a wish too.
May your wish and my wish both come true.
I go to school and have a hard time with spelling and music
But my math is just fine.
My teacher doesn't seem to know how hard I try
When I can not learn it makes me cry.

I wish a wish you'll wish a wish too.
May your wish and my wish both come true.

Ernesto Valiente
Age 13

Clinton's Rap 2

Man don't say nothing to me,
If it's not cool just let me be.
Violence starts when you tease me.
I get so mad I can't think or see.
We start to trade a punch or two,
Then someone is hurt before we're through.
So how about we get back tight,
I'd rather hang out and end this fight.
Let's be friends and work things out,
So violence can lose another bout.

Clinton Washington
Age 13

Ian's Poem

I've lived 18 years in a city of greed and sin
And been so close to the edge that many thought I'd already fallen in…

To the hate and stereotypes seen on tv.
And the negative fates which are so evident to me.

Do as I say, boy, and not as I do.
To me, simple expressions never proved so true
As lying, drug dealing politicians tell kids to stay in school
Each society, apparently has their own morals and rules
And these are the situations from which our game unfolds
Trying to turn away from everything to which we've been exposed.
And in this game we've all been trapped
Based not on who or what we are but solely where we're at.

So why not just move away?
Well, I suppose we do in our own, separate ways
Some runaway, do drugs or commit suicide
But heaven or hell, drunk or high
You still have the same pain inside
And running away has never helped a soul
Cuz ignoring the fire makes it burn out of control
Not knowing where we're going
And barely knowing where you've been
Disallows you to get comfortable
Because you know you'll have to move again.

Helping out our neighbors might begin to ease some pain
But many people seldom do things from which they won't
benefit or gain
So now the point of view by which we stand
Often leaves us unable to lend a helping hand
I've got so many problems weighing me down
And to grab yours too, might force us both to drown
So now hopefully you can see
How this game's been eating away at you and me,
And resolutions won't come into sight
Until we all join forces and are ready to fight.

Ian Atkinson
Age 18

Jasmine

Like stars twinkling in the sky
Like white roses in the garden
Where jasmines stay
Smell like perfume
Middle like twinkling diamonds
They are, of course, "yellow"
They look like they have spiky
leaves
But really are as soft as the wind

…Some of the leaves are as dry
as the hot sandy desert.

Kyra Hoge-Habekoss
Age 8

Amy Ung
Age 9

Secrets Never Shared

Secrets
Secrets never shared
Oh, God my secrets…
My secrets were never shared

There's been so much pain I've borne
Incest and rape left me a scar
A child
Left with scars never shared
My child
Was left with scars never shared

Nightmares start at early ages
And I never stopped going through the stages
The nightmares
The nightmares never shared
My nightmares
My nightmares were never shared

Yesterday gone past without a friend
But today I see them reaching out a hand
Today
Today I walk along
Today
Today I walk along with my friends

Magnolia Jackson
Age 17

Knowledge

Sitting here minding my own,
You sat there all alone
Correcting my words. Telling me I was dumb.
Old man you should have known…
What you now have started,
I have already won.

The battle of knowledge
You're old, so you're smart.
I'm you don't know nothing,
And still have a heart.

So take a look at my clothing
I'm loud and outlandish
Old man if you only knew
How much I can't stand this

So you say I have no home training
My house must be a mess
Well let me let you know now,
You can lay all that mess to rest

Now I am only 16, working on a dream

To bring me the knowledge
To get me that green….
Paper that is.

To keep my mind tight and my pockets fat
As for you old man,
I don't know where you'll be at,

So when I am in college
Fulfilling my dream,
Getting the knowledge
To bring me that green
I will think back to that bus stop
Where you were seen.

When I was sitting there on my own
And you sat there all alone
Correcting my words,
Telling me I was Dumb

Look at me now,
I have knowledge,
I have won.

Anastasia Ross
Age 16

Failure Ain't an Option

I'm runnin' out of breath
And I ain't stoppin'
If I slow down I'll lose
Failure ain't an option

I'll stop when I'm finished
And my goals are achieved
A successful individual
I know I will be

But these goals won't be reached
If my mind ain't right
Now right before I sleep
I say my prayers at night

To stay focused
And to keep runnin' the same pace
I'll receive a GED
At the end of this race

My life has been rough
Which makes it hard to breathe
But I cannot give up,
Cuz I got a word to keep.

I'm runnin out of breath
And I ain't stoppin'
If I slow down I'll lose
And failure ain't an option

Jesse Holford
Age 18

Growing Up Strong

Most of my life until I was 7 years old and put into foster care, I had to be the parent, with 2 mamas, 4 uncles, 8 cousins, and 5 out of 10 of my mama's children, all in the same house. I had to take on the responsibilities. On a typical day,

I would get up each morning,

wake up my cousins who were all younger than me,

get them dressed,

comb their hair the best way I knew how,

steal enough money from my uncle so we could get doughnuts and milk
　　　　on the way to school,

drop my cousins off at daycare,

then walk to my school.

When I'd get off from school,

I'd pick up my cousins from their school,

take them to the park,

feed them some free lunch meals I had taken from school,

go home, make sure we did our homework,

make sure we took our baths,

wash their clothes in the bath tub for the next day,

And then, at last, play in the room until we fell asleep.

That was my everyday routine....

While my mama and uncles handled whatever business they had,

we were all on our own. And even though I was only 7 years old,

I had to learn from my experiences anyway,

learn to be responsible, and independent,

and know what I need to do to take care of myself.

There are so many young people like myself who have gone through the same thing,

who have been abandoned and abused,

who have not EVER had a voice,

and who don't always make it.

And soon we start to get older and older, witnessing the shootings that happen everyday with no one being blamed. We get older and older watching the drugs being passed from hand to hand as we walk down the streets with no one getting caught.

And as we get older, we internalize the negative illustrations,

And think this is how life should be lived.

So we start acting out in order to be seen and to be heard.

Some youth feel that there are no other choices but to kill, steal, and sell drugs. This is how we think even though it shouldn't be like this. We do it anyway. Even though all we see on the street corners and in the houses we grow up in are violence and abuse, we don't realize that we can change our lives starting within ourselves.

When I was growing up I lived around all kinds of shootings,

all kinds of drugs,

But it didn't mean I had to sell drugs because my uncles did.

It didn't mean that I had to start stealing

just because all my cousins did.

It didn't mean I had to start shooting up crack because my aunties did.

WHAT MATTERS IS, I am my own person,

and I learned that at seven years old.

if I wanted something to be done, I had to do it myself because no one else will do it for me. I told myself that I was never gonna be like the people I live with, and today, I am not, because I was strong, and I kept my head up.

In order to reach my goal of not wanting to be like them,
I did the opposite.
They sold drugs, I sold newspapers.
They were shooting each other, I was shooting basketball hoops.
When the prostitutes came laying up in my uncles' beds,
I was laying in my bed asleep.

Today, I'm going to school.
I got a job.
I go to church.
I sing in the choir.
I don't need to sell and get high off drugs.
I get high off myself and the positive things I do.

I don't need to fight with you.
Don't mean I can't fight if I want to stoop down to that level.
I'm not a trouble maker. Don't make trouble with me.

SO WHAT MATTERS IS, when you see me on the street (girl), no need to pull your purse a little closer
to you. See me as a strong black woman. I don't need your money. Don't try me for a poor little black girl
with nothin' for a future. *I will make my future.*
And yes, if it sounds like I got an attitude…LISTEN…
I NEED to be heard because
I'M THE VOICE FOR THE VOICELESS.

Classy Martin
Age 18

My Heart Will Go On

My heart will go on,
My heart has to go on as I sit here
Remembering about the past,
When I really should be looking at the future
Oh no, can you hear it?
My heart is pounding 10 times faster,
Faster then usual
Faster, faster, faster
It pounds
Suddenly, it stopped.
What the hell just happened?

I asked the doctor
You were in a daze from smoking all that damn killa
Girl you better stop while you're ahead
Because next time I guarantee you dead
Now straighten up your act
And you won't have to worry about your heart
Cause like I said, next time you're dead
And don't worry about going to hell,
Because you're already there
Just follow your heart to wherever it might be
Just stay right there with it like your mother was
There your heart will go on
My heart will too when I see you
Walk across that stage on graduation day
Yes your heart will go on
If you straightened up here   right now
Your heart will go on for centuries
And eventually you'll die
Not because of weed
But because you earned your wings

Dana Johnson
Age 16

You are Like the Rain

You are like the rain falling from the sky,
Helping me to get through the hard times.
Because you give me what I need…
I can grow through the weeds,
And blossom into the sunlight.

Dawn Moananu
Age 14

...the day will come when all God's...
...black to treble white will be significant
...stitutions keyboard.

Martin Luther King, Jr.
San Francisco, 1956

José Estrella
Age 10

Written With a Pen

Written with a pen
Sealed with a Kiss
If you are my friend
Please answer this

Are you my friend, or are you not?
You told me once,
But I forgot

If I die,
Before you do
I would go to heaven
And wait for you

I'll give the angels back their wings
And risk the loss of everything…

Just to prove my friendship is true.

I like having someone

Just like you

Classy Martin
Age 16

There's a Killer on the Loose

For all the young folks
Around this town let me turn you on
To what's coming down.
There's a killer on the loose.
There's a killer on the loose.

Ain't got no gun,
No knife, no rope.
It can get in your veins
If you're shooting dope.

There's a killer on the loose.
There's a killer on the loose.

Although they say wait
'cause you're too young
I gotta admit
Sex sure is fun.
Ok. Go on and have fun
With your "hon"
But you could die
Without a condom.
He's so cute, she's so fine
Sleeping with everybody
You lay your life on the line.

There's a killer on the loose
There's a killer on the loose.

Makes no difference
If you're straight or gay
This crazy killer
Is gonna have its way.
I know you're wondering
"well what's its name",
this bad killer that's giving such pain?
Open your eyes
Let me show you the way
This killer of killers
Goes by the name of AIDS.
AIDS is the killer on the loose.

Take care to read
All you can
About this killer
Of woman and man.

Tell friends and family
And enemies too
We're gonna waste AIDS
Before we're through.

By all of us working
On the same team
AIDS can be just another bad dream.

Stop the killer on the loose
Stop the killer on the loose.

Anthony and JJH Hayes
Age 16

Darell Davis
Age 10

...Why did it

take a gun

to give this boy

a voice...?

–Tiarra

Visionary, Not a Dreamer

I hate writing papers about Dr. King's dream.
Dr. King was a visionary, not a dreamer.
I am also tired of everyone but black people winning the Martin Luther King contest.
What are the people looking for who judge the contest?

The best writers?
Who can put a period at the end of a sentence?

I am a young black man who is hurting because of Dr. King's dream.
I am a young black man who has grown beyond what others expect,
because of visionaries like Dr. King.
I dream of having a family and home.

I have lived in five homes in the last four years.
I dream of having a school and friends,
but I have been in six schools in five years.
I have dreamed about going to sleepovers
and going to parties and inviting my friends over.
All I ever hear is you can't do this, you can't do that,
because you are a foster kid.
Is this Dr. King's dream for me?
Where are the carriers of the visions of Dr. King?
Do you carry my soul and life in your vision?
Dr. King was not a dreamer; he was a visionary.
I was not in his dream in 1963, and I will not win any contest.
But I was in Dr. King's vision of a future for all children.

Clinton Washington
Age 13

A 13 Year Old Boy

A 13 year-old-boy stole a .22 caliber pistol
And shot up his school cafeteria
He climbed on the table and fired one shot at the ceiling.
All of the children at the middle school were terrified
As the young boy yelled: "get to the stage right now, or I'll
Kill all of you!"

Why did it take a gun
To give this boy a voice?

I think something terrible happened in his life,
And it was not talked out…
So his way of talking it out was by acting out.

We need to listen to young people more.

Tiarra Jade McLemore
Age 14

A Messed Up World

A young woman sits in the streets asking for money
People passing by giggle as if it were funny
Little do they know she has three children living in a hotel
No food, no kitchen, the daddy's in jail
He was selling drugs to support his family
But his background is not what the police want to see
I GUESS IT'S JUST A MESSED UP WORLD.

A child hides in the closet afraid of getting beat by her father,
Crying because of a broken leg is her brother
The father takes a broom stick and beats the young child
He doesn't know what he did wrong so he runs around wild
The mother doesn't care as long as she has her drugs
She sits in the corner all day killing bugs
No food, but drugs stored in the cabinets
They have so many roaches they consider them pets
I GUESS IT'S JUST A MESSED UP WORLD.

A teenage girl is remembering her mother and how she died
Every night, all night she cried
Her father never talked about it, so she kept her feelings inside
She had to face it, her mother isn't there to guide
The funeral was long and her father didn't bother to cry
And until this day she just doesn't know why
I GUESS IT'S JUST A MESSED UP WORLD.

A Teenage guy has parents who let him do whatever
That's why he didn't *mean* to get pregnant with her
He didn't know what to do so he left her with the baby.
Will this baby survive? I don't know…maybe.
Poor boy he was only 15 years old
He joins a gang thinking he's bold
He gets shot at 17, still just a kid
I can't believe I saw what I did
I GUESS IT'S JUST A MESSED UP WORLD.

Anastasia Ross
Age 17

Abuse and We Ain't Havin' It

Verbal abuse, abuse
People telling other people what to do
Or where to be
Lying in their faces
When they're in the same situation
She tells me,
Don't tell me nothing.
You help yourself before you try to help me
Damn, what the hell is going on in the world
When a woman and a man's in a physical fight.
Stop them, I cried out
As I sat there and watched them angrily
It's wrong, you stupid sissy.

Dana Johnson
Age 16

How I Feel About Violence

Everyday that I turn on the news
It makes me feel sad and blue
I know I'm tired of hearing about violence...
How about you?

Violence makes me uncomfortable
In everyway
Play fighting, putdowns, are still the same

okay?

I dream of a violent free world
With kindness, compassion and love
Smiles everyday
And praising our Lord above.

Rain of Candy
Clouds of Joy
That's every child's dream

So when you see or hear of violence
Think of this… "silence."

Recco Miguel Darcell Payne
Age 10

Two Boys Were Fighting

Two boys were fighting on a bus. One shot the other.
There were little kids on the bus when the shots were fired.

How did this child get a gun?

Why did he think violence would solve his problems?

As we ask these questions
One child is dead
And the other behind bars wondering…

What is the solution?

Let peace begin with me.

Tiffany Haynes
Age 17

This World is Upside Down

This world is upside down.
We chop down trees
We're scared of bees
We go sneeze, sneeze
When we smell flowers
We have no power
Every 5 seconds someone is dying
Every 5 seconds someone is crying
And it's very, very sad
And it makes me mad
To know every 5 seconds
Someone has to go.

Erika Sheppard
Age 11

Violence

Shot in the head with a gun.

Run,
            The violence has begun.
Gangs fighting one another in the streets,
Don't look back
Before you get beat.

Don't harass me
I don't want to fight…
you can be right.

Wait, what is happening to us?
All this violence is a disgust.
Aren't we friends?
Aren't we supposed to be family?
Can't we talk?

The violence has got to end.

I want to live in a community,
Of love, peace,
And unity.

Classy Martin
Age 16

José Estella
Age 10

Child Abuse

I sit and look at all the kids standing there
Getting beat for no reason… for no reason at all
Getting slapped around, kicked around
Getting beat until they cannot move anymore
Suffering from the beating of a monster
Suffering to stay alive and to keep their heads up high
Not low
Although they are hurt, beaten almost to death
They can make it, they can do it because…

Tiffany Haynes
Age 16

Violence Is All Kinds Of Things...

Violence is all kinds of things such as shooting,
and selling drugs. Violence is not just being violent,
but providing something that may lead to violence.
Violence can affect different people in different ways.
It can be caused by misunderstanding because it feels like
they can be understood by doing violent things. I think
that society can not help stop violent crimes by simply
just putting people in jail. We need to try and understand
their problems which lead to violence. There should
people doing more counseling sessions for people that need help.

Regina Smith
Age 12

Violence on TV

In my community…
There are people getting hurt

Because
They are watching too much violence on TV

When they try to do what people are doing on TV
They get hurt by the police and go to jail

When they go to jail they get hurt again…

But maybe they will know how others feel when they hurt them.

Monica Reece
Age 9

Sophia Valiente
Age 14

Voices

Bad:

It's time to knock him out
So aim for his face
Nah, forget it, cuss him out
And put him in his place
Call him a punk, call him a ho
Hurt his feelings and let him know
That you are not the one to be messed with
Because you will go toe to toe

Good:

Come on Jess, don't buy into that
Listen to me
Say sorry about that- shake hands
Then turn around and leave

Bad:

Oh, he is back
And look what happened
You scared him so bad
That he went and got a weapon
He came back with the club
A device to prevent stolen cars
Tell him to swing
See if he really has the heart
If he doesn't swing, leave
And look for a weapon
Then come back to teach his ass
A little lesson

Good:

Jesse it ain't that serious
Walk away
You made that man furious
Just walk away
You really can't do anything
Somebody's going to witness
Like I said walk away
And mind your business

Bad:

Hit him with the bottles
Beat him down until he's bloody
When he finally drops- forget the cops
Take his money

Good:

If you would have listened to me in the first place
And knocked him out
You would have been locked up with another case
And can't get out
Besides you went to jail for that
The second time
Trapped in a cage
You want to do that another time?

Isolated from the world
Reading books and bibles
You are only free in your dreams
But it's hard to keep your eyes closed
Stressing off when you are going to go
And leave that place

But that was in the past
Everybody makes mistakes
Now you are off of probation
Working two jobs
Almost through with school
PLEASE DO NOT
Allow this stranger
Take you to the past
You got to control your anger
You may get another chance
So throw the bottles
You know you like the sound of broken glass
Keep walking a straight path
You don't have to repeat the past

Jesse Holford
Age 18

...Somebody
needs to stop
and
pay attention...

–Classy

There's A Place

There is a place where there is life.
There is a place where there's love
There is a place where there is creatures.
There is a place where there's hatred.
There is a place where there is life
And it's called Earth and I love it.

Troy Talton
Age 10

Create a World

Create a world where
　　　　Bigotry and hatred crumble
Let peace begin with me
　　　　Where hatred and rejection and exclusion turn to love,
　　　　Acceptance, and justice.
Let peace begin with me.
　　　　Where the earth is honored, and young people
　　　　Are nurtured,
Let peace begin with me.

Jesse Holford
Age 18

Peace

Peace to me is home and good fun
and friends and sisters.
Peace means feeling safe.
My family brings me peace.
I bring myself peace from within.

Lynn Stills
Age 7

José Estella
Age 10

The Young Children in Africa

The young children in Africa are dying of AIDS.
1,800 babies a day are born with HIV.
 Families are being torn apart by this disease.

Can this war be won?
How can we make it end?

Somebody needs to stop and pay attention.

Somebody needs to spread education.

Let peace begin with me.

Classy Martin
Age 16

Peace Means to Me

What peace means to me
is to get along with everyone of different colors
which means diversity–
It's one big unity.

Peace to me is also
not fighting with each other.
It's living without the wars
and the hatred and violent acts.

Can we all just get along?

Dana Johnson
Age 16

There Is A War Going On

I just looked around
And what did I see
A kid dying on the streets
Just like me

With guns handed out like
Summer flies
Homies don't care
Who lives or dies
There is a WAR going on

Just walking down the street
Minding my own
Gun shots ring out
As a dope head shouts
There is a WAR going on

This is crazy
We ain't in IRAQ
We're in Oak Town
Man I better watch my back
There's a WAR going on

I want to grow up
So do those kids in Iraq
Have a family and a car
Now that's fact
This crazy world is really
whack

There is a WAR going on
You OG's sitting out there
Can you promise this world
Will still be there?
FOR ME
There is a WAR going on!

Ernesto Valiente
Age 13

José Estella
Age 10

American Society

Do you ever ask yourself, "Is America for me?"

Is it for me? I'm not sure.
America is supposed to be equal opportunity
and equal rights for all.

The Declaration of Independence! Ha! Please…
That was only made for the White man to succeed.

Does it apply to you?

Not to me.
> Where are the women of different races?
> Where are our faces on tv?
> Or in the fashion magazines?
> Who still owns the media?
> Who are the leaders?
> What color are they?
> Who gets the highest pay?

Do you know how many people,
How many children, how many babies,
Have lost their cultures and their pride from being assimiliated in the American Society?

America is supposed to be the land of opportunity
But yet our opportunities are limited, like the spaces
in a parking lot –
Privileged space for limousines, but for my little car…
No vacancy.

They say education is our way out
>   Of poverty
>   Of ignorance
>   Of the neighborhood

They say education is the way to be "good"

But education is only designed to teach you how to fit in a white man's world. Survive.

America will do no more for me.
I will not depend on this society
This "America"… the white man's!

I was not given a silver spoon nor fed with it.

Nothing but my bare hands to carve my way through this society.
Depend on no one else but yourself,
your community,
and your family.

I will survive
And I will take my Pride.

Is America for You?
It will be for me!

Ian Atkinson
Age 18

Celebrating Women

We celebrate women because they accomplish great things in life

We celebrate the men behind the women, like Cecil Williams,

We celebrate women like

Lena Horne, who was a great performer, and taught us how to grow more beautiful at any age.
Like Maya Angelou who told us no matter how low people put us, we still rise.
Like Oprah Winfrey who celebrates the everyday pain and joy of women.
Joyce who saves our lives by building us a home and gives us love.
Jan who is our poetry inspiration and who tells us to be ourselves.

We celebrate women like

Rosa Parks and Harriet Tubman, Sojourner Truth and
Hillary Clinton, Isabel Allende and Selena.

Maxine Hong Kingston and Dolores Huerta,
Women of all Red Nations,
Women of all ages and ethnicities and sexual orientations
And
Disabilities.

Women who survive cancer and poverty and war
Abuse, violence, harassment, and discrimination

To all the women who prove that we can be independent

We celebrate all of you every day!!!!

Melissa Quinteros
Age 15

Why Did You Do What You Did?

i wanna know why you did what you did
was it because i was a mental kid
did you take my heart and fill it with pain
yeah you took my love and more pain I gained
why did you say i was your little one
that made my feelings go hide and run
was i so hopeless that you could just hurt me
then later in the end just totally desert me
what did i do to be hurt at fifteen
my life had just begun my future i could see
was i so hopeless 'cause i was young and confused
that it wouldn't matter if i was hurt or abused
what was my weakness i lived in fear
you masturbated me but i didn't shed no tear
i lost my virginity maybe not to you
but you hurt me bad like the others had too
you stole my virginity what little i had
you made me feel helpless and my heart very sad
you made me do horrible things that hurt me deep down
but i repressed the feelings as i traveled through town
you said you'd teach me what real love was about
but instead deep down you made my heart shout
i was emotionally disturbed so what did i do
to deserve the hurt that i was given by you
i was only fifteen years old but mentally i was a kid
that's why i wanna know why you did what you did

Magnolia Jackson
(aka) Kathryn Onarah Everett
Age 16

With All Due Respect

With all due respect to you, Dr. King
I regret to inform you that we're not living your dream
And anyone with eyes open knows just what I mean
Racism is rampant, segregation exists
People commit hate crimes while blinded by their own prejudice

With all due respect, we may be further than ever
Though I wasn't around back then, things today can't be much better
The only thing different about racism is that now people deny it
Sell excuses for their actions; but me, I don't buy it.
Growing up in the city I see how it goes
When whites and blacks walk together, they're forced to stay on their toes
People have stunned me with their look as they walk by
Hate, fear and confusion just fills up their eyes

So with all due respect, we're still real far away
And for every person trying to help, two more stand in the way
People propose resolutions, then go back on their word
Then try to make sure the people who speak up for change are not heard

And with all due respect, your life supports such a case
You spoke of love and equality, something people tried to erase
But what they didn't know is that you'd already planted the seed
And for many still alive today that's all we need

With all due respect your dream's not yet been achieved
But hope's kept alive because we still believe.

Ian Atkinson
Age 18

Ernesto Valiente
Age 13

In Los Angeles

A police officer sees his fellow officer
Shoot and kill a homeless woman, Margaret Mitchell.

The officer said he shot her because she charged at him
With a screw driver.

Her family is suing the city of Los Angeles.

I wonder
what the police could have done
besides shoot
the woman?

Did he tell her to drop her weapon?
Some homeless people have mental illnesses
And other problems like being angry...
I wish the officers could have helped her,
Talked to her about going to the hospital
Before they had to kill her.

Tiffany Haynes
Age 16

Women of God

I hate the man who knows it all
And I don't know nothing cause I am a girl
Yes, I am a girl and I don't know nothing about no bible
And the man's interpretation must be the cure
Hope, I am just the nurturer, the moral guardian
I only bear your sons
But I don't know nothing about no love, or care, or creation
Hope, I just sit here and listen to your shit
Called religion that has nothing to do with living
I watch you chop down trees and
Pour cement all over Gods land
While I and my daughters deplete from our calloused hands
But I don't know nothing and I suppose
       Neither will she
Hope, she'd just lay there dead
With her legs open and her eyes closed
Wishing away the insecurities
You plaster all over billboards
But she don't know nothing about
Why her hair is falling out
After the chemical destruction of a
Child in her belly and she can't find
Self-forgiveness for the inability to feed it
Without the man's need to support the woman
We just have his creations

Hope, we don't know nothin'
Cause we are women
Women of love
Women of God
Yes, created by God
Driven to addictions and suicides
From the man's self centered obesity
Because they must know everything
And kill the unknown
And if not they kill your souls
With slavery and ideas of
 How life is supposed to be
And God forbid we speak
For we are just women
And we don't know anything
Hope, we are just women
Helpless, useless, dreadful women
Who run around trying to save lives
The destruction of Earth by men
We live the deeds of love and righteousness
With our children, and gardens, and food, and homes
Yup, we are just women
Women of Love,
Women of God
Women of God
Women of Goddess

Lucinda Ray
Age 18

Inmates

Inmates in North Carolina minimum security prison
Are building houses.
They are paid ten cents an hour…
People are buying these homes for $35,000.
It is said that the houses are terrific.

I ask, what are the rights of the prisoners?
I know that some of these prisoners have committed
terrible crimes.
And some prisoners are even innocent.
But they receive next to nothing for their hard work.

Prisoners who work should get paid fair wages.
The money should be put into a savings account for them,
Or sent to help their families at home.

Dijoun Elarms
Age 13

Piano

I can't touch
the piano
forgive me
for touching
the piano
It won't
happen again

Alex Burke
Age 11

Crystal Hayden
Age 15

6

...Lonely is when you

get a double scoop of ice cream

and the first scoop

falls over...

–Cameron

Church

My church is all religions,
Any color, no fights
Anybody black or white
You and you
Come gather around
You and you
Come dance to the sound

Erica Sheppard
Age 11

Ernesto Valiente
Age 13

Lonely

Lonely is when you are in a room
With a whole bunch of people
And there is no one to talk to.

Lonely is when you get a double scoop of ice cream
And your first scoop falls over.

Lonely is when you fall in an ever-lasting pit
Lonely is when you don't have any brothers or sisters

Lonely is when you don't know who is really your friend
And sometimes you think to yourself
Do I really belong here?

Lonely is when you are at school
And children pick on you.
And they call you names like ugly,
Bitch, and fucker.

Lonely is when people call you names
And there is no one to tell.

Lonely is when your favorite uncle dies
And you don't know why.

Lonely is when you start to get depressed
Then right at that exact moment
Your mother comes along
And says 'there is friend on the phone for you'.

And you get on the phone with your friend
And he says 'meet me at my house.'
You go to your friend's house
Open up the door, a sudden shock,
And a surprise and everyone is screaming
'surprise' and 'happy birthday'.

Then after all of that
I wasn't lonely at all.
This is the best birthday party
I've ever had.
So my point is that no one
Deserves to be lonely.

Cameron Weaver
Age 12

Sisters On The Corner

Sisters on the corner,
Did you ever get a hug
did you ever know your father
or feel your mamma's love?
Did your sidewalks glow like diamonds,
or turn to raisins in the sun?
Was your playground full of friends
and all you knew was fun ?

Or did you wake up crying
wishing daddy was around
or mama would stop drinking
when another man let her down.
And you wouldn't wake up hungry
cause the money has been spent,
and you knew about the crack –
where the money went.

Sisters on the corner
before your pain began
before the party ended
before the drugs stepped in
if you had found a someone
to help you on your journey
towards who you wanted to be.

My sisters on the corner
you may not agree
but now I see you
As a message to me.
To find a great healer and learn to heal
To find a great builder and learn to build.
To find sisters who know the world can be laughter
And from the corner is what I am after.

Adriana Hayter
Age 14

School

School is like rain falling down on me,
Rain makes me feel safe.
All I can hear are kids and teachers.
The walls are pale white, and the floor is dirty
The kids are all different colors and shapes and sizes.
It always smells like pencils.
Pencils smell like lead, sharp lead with a big eraser on top.
All the teachers are loveable;
The ones that you can talk to when you're down or blue
The ones that you can talk to about everything you want to
Just like you would talk to your mother
With respect and know you can trust her,
even if you like someone,
They will keep it a secret.
Shh…Keep it one!

Patrice Moananu
Age 12

Crystal Hayden
Age 15

Sharks

They have a dorsal fin.
Their upper and under body is white.
Their eyes are rainbows.
My Shark is a girl. They are scary too.

Ashley Haynes
Age 10

Sports and Church

Sometimes I do sports
It is good
Church is where I learn
I love church!!
I really love church!!
I have the best mentor there.
I love doing my thing
With love that is so powerful
The Lord is good to me
Be helpful to homeless and others
I want to be strong
So I love to do something every time
I want to be strong.

Recco Payne
Age 11

Untitled

My heart beats
I count them
...and how many time the ball bounces
hard breathing
the foul
the points

The losses
the wins
I love the feel
of the basketball
the rush
the fun

It calls to me
like music
but they are not
da same cuz
b-ball
is a different game.

Christina Calloway
Age 11

George Briggs
Age 10

Pimp Car

Bright
Red
Gold
Rims
Switches
Leather
Seats
Stacks
of
money.
Pimp

Dominic Valiente
Age 10

Dripping Honey

Black eyed peas and sushi
Tacos, Nachos, Broccoli
Is how I see my family.

Special corners of my room
       Hold memories
Of tootsie rolls and gummi bears
Mommy and Daddy being there
Together smiling

       Before the storm

Blew them apart after I was born

Chocolate kisses dance all day
To keep the sadness far away
Sade, Italy, Angelic, Aasiya
Crowd my life with so much pleasure
Volleyball, choir, music and reading
Take the place of a heart that's bleeding

Cecil Williams empowers us all
He brings us up when we might fall

Thank you Glide

Unknown

Something I Hadn't Noticed Before

I looked on the street and saw something
I hadn't noticed before.

A mother and her son
Asking everyone
For spare change
The boy's face was dirty
The momma was sad,
Hair uncombed
Their life looking bad.

What had they done
to deserve living like this?
They were poor homeless,
Looking forward to nothingness.

Asking for food
Their eyes say,
"sorry to intrude on your day…
you average, normal girls who are like me…"
We think we got problems until we see

Something we hadn't noticed before.

A mother and her son
They holler for a dollar
Just to stay alive.

I see no one wants to help,
Head turned, walking by,
Can't we reach out, can't we try?

It can happen to us, becoming poor…
And we can turn into the nothingness
That we hadn't noticed before.

Classy Martin
Age 16

My World Feels Unsafe

I look at the world and I don't feel safe.
To live safely I have to find a different place.
The only place I can go where no one enters my mind
That way no one of any sort, any kind
Will be able to find what is mine.
The crack heads on the corner,
Guns shooting off with no one to warn you
I look around and what do I see?
Old ass men trying to get at me

Patrice Moananu
Age 12

My Neighborhood

My neighborhood is not perfect,
But really no neighborhood is.
There are people drunk and passed out
on the street.
There are cars running red lights, crashes,
fights, fires.
There are mothers and fathers who don't
Even know if they'll see their children later on that
evening.
There are children playing and learning
new things.
There are playgrounds and hangout places.
My neighborhood isn't perfect and then
again no neighborhood is.

Cierra Crowell
Age 10

José Estella
Age 10

Forgive

I remember when I was ten years old, living in Cambodia, when my father was drunk and took all the food from the house. I was so hungry. I went to the fruit tree of the neighborhood and ate the fruit. My big brother saw me and took me to my father. He was so mad, he kicked me and hit me with a stick. He told me to go away because I was no longer his son. So I went away and never came back home. I lived in the streets for three years, and half of my body was paralyzed. But God had shown me the way, because later on, I met Phyllis.

After we knew each other for about a month, she asked me to be her son. Nine months later, I came to America. I went to school to learn English. I had some operations to help me be more mobile. I lived with my American family, and was adopted by them. I have a happy life now.

In 1999, I visited Cambodia with my adopted mother and father, Phyllis and Michael. They had a wonderful time. It was all different than before. My biological father was especially different because of his drinking. He now has lost the spirit of his life. But the good thing was that he still remembered my name. When I saw him, I did not feel anger. I was so happy to see him and he was happy to see me too. I had learned a lot since I came to America because I put the feeling of love inside my mind and heart, not the hatred and bad memories. I cannot still be mad at him, because life is too short. Even though he had done bad things to me, I still forgive him by loving and respecting him as my father. I gave him some money to buy food, and I bought a color TV for him and hooked it up to a car battery, since he had no electricity.

Just like in the Bible, God says that the person that has done bad things to us still should not be thrown away. We must pray for them and God will show them the way and forgive them.

Samnang Em Kaplan
Age 16

I Don't Want to Live by This Stuff

Riding down the street
Looked to my right
I see a dude break dancing
I stop to take a look
I was just standing there
Like a bee looking at a beehive
Then some fools rolled up drinking beer
They got in my way
I asked them to move
But they didn't move
I do not want to live by this stuff
So I bounced out of that joint
And rolled down the street
Minding my own

Ernesto Valiente
Age 13

School

long
fun
crowded

teachers
kid
learning

fights
classes
talking

halls
lockers
books

school

Morgan Turner
Age 14

Cadillac

cool
tite
weird
sweet
taste
sick
wicked

Alex Burke
Age 11

Mauricio Rangel
Age 10

Dear Teacher,   October 14, 1982

Teacher, you sent me to the Dean 'cause I been bad
But I'm mad 'cause the memories is making me sad
I don't mean to scream and give you hard times
But kids are human too/ we got problems in our young minds
You say I am smart and if I use my head I will pass
The first thing I need to do is stop sleeping in your class
But teacher–I can't fall asleep in my house
So many perpetrators always running in and out
Brown pipes that cut like butcher knives? I see them in my mind
dark holes with black grass? I'd rather sleep in your class

Teacher–School is a safe place
Friends try to comfort me and no adults try to sneak and rape
At home when I'm sleeping, brown pipes push into my thighs
I start weeping, but mom can't hear my cries
She is in another room nursing her drug habit
I wish she could love me instead, but she's gotta have it
I wanna tell her everything but I fear for my life
I tried to tell her one time and she beat me with a pipe
I know I am smart and can pass English
But I am haunted by the things I am seeing
Everyday it seems the memories is growing stronger
I'm scared as hell and can't take it any longer

Trying to pull an "A" in your class? It's a mystery
Between the memories and the studying, I'm going crazy
I toss in my chair and pull out my hair
I see the memories everywhere but nobody seems to care
I get to class and go insane thinking about them creeps
I just wanna crawl in bed and have no one wake me from my sleep
I wish I could live at school because it's so much better
Than my own home/at school I don't feel alone

Teacher–If I make you mad–I don't mean to
I wanna make you proud, teacher–honest to God I do
Writing is my form of art and I'm writing this from my heart
Please listen/please pay attention
Maybe for once you can listen to me explain
Instead of thinking I'm trying to drive you insane
Because I never mean to give you a hard time
But I am only human too/ I got problems on my young mind

Magnolia Jackson
Age 14

Packing My Bags

Packing my clothes, shoes, toys, etc. in my bags
I don't know why…

But I obeyed what my mother said

At the last minute she told me
"We're moving"

I didn't understand why
She didn't reply
She just walked away and said nothing

Then it hit me
She was sad that we were leaving

When we moved into our new house
With all our old stuff
I realized it felt just like home

Then I found out that packing my bags isn't that bad.

Anonymous

Overrated Luxuries

I prefer a house that feels like home
Rather than a shallow mansion
I prefer silver that shines shimmer
Than the dull yellow of gold
Flannel pajamas and cotton sheets
Much better than a heater
Old Navy blue jeans
Than Banana Republic sweatshirts
I prefer smiles over
Exaggerated laughs
Love out of sincerity
Rather than perfection

Lucinda Ray
Age 18

Thank You For My Home

Thank You for my Home
Where smiles are
flying around like
butterflies

and I can touch a
floor that is mine

Diane Crowder
Age 12

Sweat Lodge

As I sat in the sweat lodge
With sweat running down my hot, steaming face
I was thinking of what I could pray about
When it's my turn
It felt like I was in heaven
Because God was there
And so were all of my ancestors
I could feel their cold breath running down my back
As the men brought in seven more steaming rocks
It got hotter and hotter
And as the medicine woman put more sage on the rocks
It smelled holy
Finally it was time to leave and get some rest

Patrice Moananu
Age 13

What I See

In my neighborhood I see…

People getting shot.
I see homeless people being beaten
and mistreated for no reason at all.
I see gangs and guns all around.
I see bad men spray on the walls,
the ground
and poles.
Police arrest the bad men…
And bust in their doors and apartment windows.

These are the things that I see.

Richard Smith
Age 7

What If...

What if I'm late for school?
What if they closed the pool?
What if I get beat up?
What if they put poison in my cup?
What if I cry?
What if I get sick and die?
What if I flunk a test?
What if green hair grows on my chest?
What if no one likes me?
What if I get struck by lightening?
What if I grow taller?
What if my head gets smaller?
What if they start a war?
What if my parents get divorced?
What if?

Dawn Moananu
Age 14

When I Cry

When I cry my feelings are hurt,
I'll be walking down the street
See this little girl come up to me
And ask me, "Do you have any change?"
And I'm sitting here about to cry
And I say, "I don't have any change."
So she cries
And her mom hits her
So I cry harder.
Then I walk down the street
And I think this town is full of poor people
How sad
And I see this lady. She is smelly
But it ain't my problem
So I wave my hand across my nose
And she cusses me out
So I cry.

I cry cause I see this little girl
Get helped and the mom got cleaned up
So I cry. I cry because I am happy.
I cry because you are a healthy mother
To your daughter
Who almost died.
She had a disease
And you treated her right.
You can cuss me out for crying
But remember, you made it!
So I cry. Cry.
And I am still crying.
Why?
Because you made it
So I cry

Pearlie Martin
Age 12

177

We Pray for the Kids

We pray for the kids who live life on the edge
We pray for the kids who are doped up on meds
We pray for the kids too scared to sleep in their beds
We pray for the kids, Lord let them rest their weary heads.
We pray for the kids who experience defeat
Who don't have a home, no food to eat
So they come to Glide, where everything's all right
They know they're loved here, all day and all night.
We pray for the kids who live life in fear
For the kids who taste nothing but their salty tears
We pray for the kids who are no longer here
We pray for these kids year after year.
We pray for the kids who get beat at home
Who get locked inside closets and left alone
We pray for the bruised and the broken bones
We pray for the abuser to set a new tone.
We pray for the healing of all the above
We pray they have strength, friendship and love
We pray that these kids get through all the strife
So that they can begin to live a healthy life.
Lord keep teaching us to hear these prayers
Lord let these kids know that someone cares.

Anastasia Ross
Age 18

Cheery Wong
Age 9

Keeping the Dream Alive

I keep the dream alive by
kissing my mom every day.
I keep the dream alive by
brushing my hair, washing my face
and going to school to learn.

I keep the dream alive by saying
my prayers and trying to be good.
I keep the dream alive by going to
Church and giving people hugs.

I want to write stories when I grow
up that people will read.
I can keep Dr. King's dream
Alive by helping others
and by loving my family.

Dominic Valiente
Age 10

My Life in the Hotel

There was anger, anger everywhere.
The space so small it grew on you
People getting so mad at each other
You can't think straight.
No room to breathe. No room to be me.
I was so ashamed to live in that place.

That hotel,
It is no place for a kid to be.

My new life at Cecil Williams Community House
I have my own room, my own room.
It is so quiet! I have my own Space.
I get smiled at a lot. People like me now.
I feel normal. I feel important.

I don't have to be ashamed any more.

La'Teisha Brathwaite
Age 12

They Are The Ones Who

They are the ones who help us
When the tide doesn't wash our way,
They explain to us what went astray,
They comfort us through bad times and hold our hand in need,
They are like the apple of our life and the water of our tree,
They let us know they're always there when no one else can help
And let us know who's real for us,

Family is the ones that let us know the real,
They explain to us and help us as we say what we feel
And when they're not helping or seeing us through
And when we're not seeing they're watching our step
To see if we're on the right path,
To see if we're going the route that will guide us,

A map for our life,
A key for our day,
There's an answer to our strife,

Families are the ones that help us,
We can always turn to them,
An extra petal that's on our leaf,
The guidance in our life when we turn to them for help,
Help us . . . .
The Glide family and ever growing Love,
The happiness we share down and up with Love
And so I say to you my friends they are the kindest people
Watch for the movie to my poem there's a sequel,
Because this poem consists of Love and will never stop growing.

Adriana Hayter
Age 13

Ernesto Valiente
Age 13

*This book was printed
through a generous gift
from the Furth Family Foundation.*